PICTORIAL CHINESE SAYINGS (6)

A Tale to Tell

(Part I)

PICTORIAL CHINESE SAYINGS (6)
A Tale to Tell
(Part I)

André Loo

Translated by
Esther Dent-Young
Ph.D. (Madrid)

SILK ROAD PRESS

Project Director: André Loo
Series Editor: Adrienne Lam
Translator: Esther Dent-Young
Illustrator: Bernadette Yan-lok Yung
Chinese Seal: Lee Wai Him
Cover Design: Cycle Advertising Ltd.

ISBN: 1-890807-05-2

Library of Congress Catalog Card Number: 97-61702

Printed in Hong Kong

To
Winifred
Joyce, Grace
and
Albert

Contents

Acknowledgments

This modest series is my own idea and it would not have taken shape without the combined efforts of my friends.

General editor for the series is Adrienne Lam.

The translator of Volumes 1, 2, 6 is Esther Dent-Young. The translator of Volumes 3, 4, 5, 7, 8 is Adrienne Lam.

The illustrations for the series were the work of Cheng Lai, Bernadette Yan-lok Yung, Clara Man-ki Suc and Fung Yuk Sung.

Chinese seals are the work of Lee Wai Him.

Ma Schum offered many valuable opinions on the content and presentation.

Matilda Wong, former lecturer in English at the City University of Hong Kong, gave valuable comments on the translation.

Transcription in Cantonese is the effort of Betty Hung, instructor in Cantonese at The University of Hong Kong.

My deepest thanks to all the above.

The Chinese relics in the photos are from the author's own collection. The photos of the scenic spots were taken by the author.

I have tried to complete this series with all due care but in any work involving two transcriptions systems, two languages and one dialect, there may exist discrepancy. These remain my own and I would be grateful for any suggestions from readers. Please write to:

Silk Road Press Inc., P.O. Box 27623, Tempe, AZ 85283-7623.

If these changes are adopted in future editions, you will receive a complimentary copy as a token of our appreciation.

How To Use This Book

PICTORIAL CHINESE SAYINGS is a set of books in eight volumes. Its modest aim is to provide interesting supplementary materials for those who are learning Chinese as well as the general reader. Through the channel of *chengyu* (成语), we hope to show them something of Chinese culture, thought and customs.

There is no exact equivalent in English for *chengyu*. Idiom, proverb, saying, expression, each conveys only one aspect of its rather comprehensive functions. In general use, the term "saying" is probably most suitable.

The role of *chengyu* in the Chinese language in writing as well as in daily colloquial use is an important one. For over two thousand years, literary gems, historical events, heroic exploits, and philosophical aphorisms have been condensed into succinct phrases, often no more than four words long. They are familiar to not only the educated class but the uneducated masses as well.

This development of the Chinese language is a linguistic phenomenon which helps to shape and enrich the speech of the entire race. In learning Chinese, acquiring a good knowledge of *chengyu* is an important step not to be overlooked by any serious student.

The selections of *chengyu* in these volumes are not classified according to any scholarly basis but by category. Those with a good story behind them are grouped into three volumes titled *A Tale to Tell*, Part I, II & III. Those involving numbers, animals, plants, nature, and the body each occupy a separate volume. Readers will find such a grouping convenient in learning related words and phrases as they can all be found in one volume.

The choice of *chengyu* naturally falls on those most frequently seen and heard. A few rarely used *chengyu* are included simply because of their literary value.

In order to make the best use of this book, please note the following:

1. By academic tradition, the order of appearance of the *chengyu* is according to the number of strokes in the first character. One stroke goes first; two strokes, second and so on. Should the number of strokes be the same, the second character is used. The exception is the volume on numbers, when it is more useful to present the *chengyu* numerically. Simplified Chinese characters are used throughout this series.

2. Two sets of transcriptions are given: Hanyu Pinyin for Modern Standard Chinese and the Yale system for Cantonese. (Please see Appendices 1 & 2) Modern Standard Chinese is the national tongue and Cantonese is the regional dialect of the southern province of Guangdong. Cantonese is widely used in Hong Kong and overseas Chinese communities.

3. For each word in a *chengyu*, the literal meaning is given in English. The literal meaning of the whole *chengyu* is also given. The idiomatic meaning and any English equivalent are provided when applicable. For example, 'shā jī qǔ luǎn' (杀鸡取卵) :

   > **Literal meaning:** to kill the chicken to get the egg
   > **Meaning:** to cause long-term harm through short-term gain
   > **English equivalent:** kill the goose that lays the golden eggs

4. The notes reflect the writer's own point of view. Some words have several meanings. If any meaning is more widely used than the one in the *chengyu*, it is included for the reader's reference. Words which may cause confusion because they are closely alike in shape or pronunciation are presented and clarified. Any related *chengyu*, synonyms and antonyms are also included, with the pinyin and meaning.

5. Words and phrases which are in popular use and closely related to words in each *chengyu* are included in the Related Vocabulary, with pinyin and meaning in English. Vocabulary set in the original complex form with Cantonese Romanization is in Appendix 4.

6. A Chronology of Chinese Dynasties appears in Appendix 3.

7. The illustration accompanying each *chengyu* is served here as a sidedish. It is hoped that it will tickle the reader's palate.

Introduction

A *Tale to Tell* is divided into three volumes each containing 35 *chengyu* of a narrative nature. They are selected for their rich symbolism and vividness.

Most of these sayings originated from the pre-Qin era, that is, 770 – 221 B C. This era of about five and half centuries is divided into two periods: Chunqiu (770 – 476 B C) and Warring States (475 – 221 B C).

These two periods saw the flourishing of Chinese learning at a level unsurpassed in later times. Practical experience combined with wisdom produced many profound works. Chinese sayings from these two periods are the crystallization of such thoughts and ideas.

The end of the monopoly on learning by government, the visits of scholars to courts of prince and lords and their service in public affairs; in short, the secularization of learning gave rise to many famous sayings pertaining to the art of war, to government administration and to diplomacy.

There are reclusive scholars who lead the life of hermits and devote themselves to writing. Some of them write allegorically, like Zhuangzi. Their writings are mines for literary quotation and aphorism. Later scholars represent the gist of a story or an essay in a four-word phrase *chengyu*, a form also employed to re-tell famous historical anecdotes.

From the Qin Dynasty to now is a period of over two thousand years which enriched the language with many *chengyu*. However, sayings from the pre-Qin era remain the most popular and influential and are still taught to every schoolchild.

To illustrate these volumes are specially commissioned cartoons with a contemporary flavour, to make these little morality tales more appealing to modern-day readers.

Chinese Sayings
Tales I

1. WORDS OF GOLD

一 字 千 金

Pinyin: yī zì qiān jīn

Cantonese: yāt jih chìn gàm

一 one
字 word
千 one thousand
金 gold

Literal meaning: one word is (priced at) a thousand pieces of gold

Meaning: a valuable article

English equivalent: a literary gem

Story: The story behind this belongs to the period from 240–200BC. Lǔ Bùwéi (呂不韋) was an astute businessman, who made a lot of money, buying cheap and selling dear. When the famous king Qín Shǐhuáng's (秦始皇) father was a hostage abroad, Lu Buwei helped him to return and become king. In gratitude Qin Shiguang later made Lu Buwei his prime minister. When Lu Buwei was prime minister he assembled a group of scholars and compiled a book of two hundred thousand words, which included history, geography, and biography. The title of this anthology was *Lǔshì Chūnqiū* (呂氏春秋) or *Lu's Spring and Autumn annals*. After the book was finished he posted it on the city gate of the capital together with a thousand pieces of gold, and announced: "If anyone by changing one word can make it more perfect, he will have this reward."

Note: *Chunqiu* (春秋) is a book by Confucius, Kǒngzǐ (孔子) (551–479 BC), recording important events during the period between 770−476 B C. This period is also designated as the Spring and Autumn Era. The acumen and sound judgement expressed in this book makes it a model for all subsequent historical writings. Books written with a *"Chunqiu pen"* is an expression of the greatest merit. Lu's book alludes to this.

'Kè zhōu qiú jiàn' (刻舟求剑) (page 32) and 'yī míng jīng rén' (一鸣惊人) (page 4) are from this source.

Related vocabulary

字典 (zìdiǎn) dictionary
字体 (zìtǐ) script; style of calligraphy
字帖 (zìtiè) copybook for calligraphy
数字 (shùzì) figure; amount
文字 (wénzì) written language
金属 (jīnshǔ) metal
黄金 (huángjīn) gold
黄金时代 (huángjīn shídài) golden age

2. SURPRISE!

一 鸣 惊 人

Pinyin: yī míng jīng rén
Cantonese: yāt mìhng gìng yàhn

一 one
鸣 cry
惊 surprises
人 people

Literal meaning: one cry startles the world

Meaning: a big surprise

English equivalent: to startle the world

Story: During the Warring States Period there was a very talented King Wēi of Qí（齐威王）who had neglected affairs of state. The whole country was going to pieces and neighboring states had begun to seize the border areas. But the ministers were too afraid of the king to say anything and the country's decline continued.

Eventually one minister, name Chúnyū Kūn（淳于髡）who knew that the king was fond of solving riddles, used the form of a riddle to say to the king: "In our country there is a big bird which has lived in the imperial palace three years and never tried to fly, never uttered a cry. It just sits there idly all day long. Who can tell what bird this is?"

The king realised this was a criticism of himself and saw at once the error of his ways. He smiled and answered: "You know this bird is not just an ordinary bird. He doesn't fly, it is true, but when he does he will fly higher than any other; he utters no cry, it is true, but when he does he will amaze the world."

From this moment the king changed his way of life. He devoted himself to state affairs and to building up his army and the country grew wealthy and strong. All the lost territory was taken back. This king became one of the strongest kings of the era.

Related vocabulary

鸣禽 (míngqín) songbird
惊动 (jīngdòng) alarm, disturb
惊慌 (jīnghuāng) frightened, alarmed
惊奇 (jīngqí) be surprised
惊天动地 (jīngtiān dòngdì) shaking heaven and earth
惊险 (jīngxiǎn) breathtaking, alarmingly dangerous
惊心动魄 (jīngxīn dòngpò) soul-stirring

3. MORALE

一 鼓 作 气

Pinyin: yī gú zuò qì

Cantonese: yāt gú jok hei

一 one
鼓 drum
作 rise
气 courage

Literal meaning: the first round of drum beats sets morale high

Meaning: to accomplish something in one stroke

English equivalent: to strike while the iron is hot

Story: During the Spring and Autumn Period, a clever strategist Cáoguì（曹刿）and his lord, Duke Zhuāng of Lǔ（鲁庄公）were resisting an enemy invasion. The two sides were drawn up facing each other. The enemy immediately started to beat the drum to sound the attack. The king wanted to respond immediately. But the strategist stopped him and told him to do nothing until the enemy had beaten the drum three times. As a result of this strategy they were victorious. Afterwards the duke asked for an explanation. The strategist answered that success in battle is all a matter of morale. "The first time the drum beats it rouses the soldiers' spirits. But if the engagement is not commenced, their courage dwindles at the second beating of the drum, and at the third it evaporates entirely. When the enemy's courage had evaporated, ours was at its height. This was the ideal moment to attack and we defeated them in one go."

Note: The story continues, and although it has nothing to do with this saying, it is worth mentioning. When the duke saw the enemy flee, he wanted to order an immediate pursuit. But again he was stopped by the strategist, who got down from the war chariot to examine the tracks of the fleeing enemy chariots. Climbing back onto the chariot, he gazed into the distance for a while. Finally he authorised the pursuit. The enemy were routed. The reason for not pursuing at once was that the enemy were powerful and might have been feigning flight in order to set an ambush and lure them to their destruction.

When the strategist saw the tracks of the retreating enemy were confused, he knew they were retreating in disorder. Some had even run off with the flag. It was clear that the enemy had been routed and it was not a trick, because a planned retreat would have been much more orderly.

In Ancient China battles were always initiated by beating a drum; if the other side had not sounded their drum you couldn't attack.

Related vocabulary

鼓励 (gǔlì) encourage, urge
鼓足干劲 (gú zú gàn jìn) to go all out
作品 (zuòpǐn) works of art and literature
工作 (gōngzuò) work
合作 (hézuò) cooperate
振作 (zhènzuò) exert oneself
气量 (qìliàng) tolerance
气派 (qìpài) manner, style, air
空气 (kōngqì) air

7

4. ACCOMPLICE

为虎作伥

Pinyin: wèi hǔ zuò chāng

Cantonese: waih fú juk chèung

为 for
虎 tiger
作 to be
伥 *chang*, spirit

Literal meaning: to help the tiger by acting as a *chang*

Meaning: to play the jackal to a tiger, to aid and abet

Story: In the forest a tiger met a man and attacked and ate him. Afterwards he wouldn't allow the man's spirit to leave. Only when the man's spirit found a second man to replace him would he be free to leave. When finally he found another victim, the spirit went and stripped him of his clothes, so the tiger could eat him more easily.

Note: East and west animism tends to separate body and soul as two independent units. When body has perished, the soul lives on.

Another saying with the same meaning is 'zhù jié wéi nüè' (助桀为虐) or 'zhù zhòu wéi nüè' (助纣为虐). Both Jie and Zhou were tyrants of ancient China and 'nüe' (虐) means tyrannize.

'Chāng' (伥) is a name of a ghost. It is said that it often stays with a tiger to do service. It is only used in modern Chinese in this saying.

'Wéi' (为) pronounced with second tone has several meanings. Please refer to "Related vocabulary".

8

Related vocabulary

为民请命 (wèi mín qǐngmìng) plead for the people

为难 (wéinían) feel embarrassed; make thing difficult for

为什么 (wèishéme) why

为生 (wéishēng) make a living

为限 (wéixiàn) not exceed

为主 (wéizhǔ) give first place to

虎口徐生 (hǔkǒu yúshēng)
  to survive a disaster,
  have a narrow escape

虎头蛇尾 (hǔtou shéwěi)
  to start well and finish
  badly

老虎 (lǎohǔ) tiger

5. LORD YE LOVES DRAGONS

叶公好龙

Pinyin: Yè Gōng hào lóng

Cantonese: Yihp Gùng hou lùhng

叶 Ye (name)

公 Gong (lord)

好 likes

龙 dragons

Literal meaning: Lord Ye loves dragons

Meaning: to pretend to like something you don't really like

Story: In ancient China there was a nobleman who liked dragons. His home was full of representations of dragons. The real dragon in the sky heard about this and wanted to thank him for being his friend, so he came down from heaven to visit. He was so big that while his head looked through the window his tail stretched to the other end of the hall. When Lord Ye saw him he was frightened out of his wits.

Note: Sometimes people explain this as pretending to love what one really fears, but this does not seem to cover all its meanings because we can also use the expression for someone who claims to love art while what he enjoys is really pornography.

In Chinese legend dragons have various characteristics: they can walk, fly or swim, they can ride on the clouds making rain. The dragon is also a symbol of the emperor. Everything belonging to the emperor can have a dragon on it, like 'lóngpáo' (龙袍) dragon robes.

"叶" used as a name is pronounced as "shè", but now all pronounce it as "yè".

When "好" is pronounced as "hǎo", it means good, fine.

Related vocabulary

落叶 (luòyè) fallen leaves
树叶 (shùyè) leaves
公有 (gōngyǒu) public
好吃 (hǎochī) tasty
好处 (hǎochu) advantage, benefit
好客 (hàokè) to be hospitable
好奇 (hàoqí) to be curious
好强 (hàoqiáng) eager to do well in everything
好人 (hǎorén) good person

6. OVERJOYED

乐 不 思 蜀

Pinyin: lè bù sī Shǔ

Cantonese: lohk bāt sì Suhk

乐 happy

不 not

思 think of

蜀 Shu (country name)

Literal meaning: being so happy he forgets the state of Shu

Meaning: to be extremely happy

Story: During the period of the Three Kingdoms, Líu Béi（刘备）the first king of Shú（蜀）died and was succeeded by his son Líu Chán（刘禅）. Liu Chan was quite stupid and the country's fortunes declined until it was annexed by Wèi（魏）. After Liu Chan's surrender he was taken to live in the capital of Wei. One day one of the leading generals of Wei gave a banquet for him, during which he ordered a performance of the songs and dances of Shu to cheer him up. All the former ministers of Shu were so moved that some of them even shed tears. Only Liu Chan went on talking and drinking unconcernedly. "Do you still miss your old country?" the general asked him. "No, not at all," Liu Chan replied. "I am very happy here, and I don't miss my country any more."

Note: A king who has lost his kingdom ought to feel sad when he is reminded of it, but Liu Chan felt nothing. It is of course possible that he was pretending, in order to allay the fears of the other side. Otherwise he must be a person without a conscience. But either way, he was able to live out his days in peace. Later in the 8th century, a poet-king in captivity was less fortunate. He did not forget his country and went on writing poems about it until his captor had him poisoned.

This saying originally had a sense of tragedy about it, but nowadays we use it simply to mean very happy, like 'lè ér wáng fǎn' (乐而忘返), so happy one forgets to go home.

The character "乐" when used to mean music is pronounced "yuè", in Cantonese "ngohk".

Related vocabulary

乐器 (yuèqì) a musical instrument
快乐 (kuàilè) happy
享乐 (xiǎnglè) to lead a life of pleasure
音乐 (yīnyuè) music
思念 (sīniàn) to think of, miss
思想 (sīxiǎng) thought, an idea

7. POOR IMITATION

东 施 效 颦

Pinyin: Dōng Shī xiào pín

Cantonese: Dùng Sì haauh pàhn

东　Dong
施　Shi
效　imitate
颦　frown

Literal meaning: Dong Shi imitate someone frowning

Meaning: to copy others blindly

English equivalent: ugly women, finely dressed, are uglier

Story: Xī Shī (西施) was a famous beauty in ancient China. One day she felt a pain in her chest and went around frowning and clutching her chest. An ugly girl next door noticed that Xi Shi still looked beautiful, even like this, so she started walking up and down the street imitating Xi Shi, frowning and clutching her chest. When the villagers saw how terribly ugly she looked, they all closed their doors and didn't want to come out. Even the poorest led their wives away to spare them the sight of such ugliness. Later people called this ugly girl Dong Shi.

Note: There is another saying with the same meaning: 'nòng qiǎo chéng zhuō' (弄巧成拙), try to be clever only to end up with a blunder.

Xi Shi was born beautiful and even if she makes an ugly face she remains beautiful. Dong Shi was ugly so when she did the same she became even uglier.

Xi Shi was a historical personage of the Spring and Autumn

Period. Dong Shi is a made-up name which plays on the contrast between "xi", west and "dong", east.

Related vocabulary

东方 (dōngfāng) the East
东西 (dōngxi) a thing
施工 (shīgōng) construction
施行 (shīxíng) to carry out
效法 (xiàofǎ) to follow an example, learn from
效果 (xiàoguǒ) result, effect
仿效 (fǎngxiào) to imitate, copy
无效 (wúxiào) of no avail, invalid

8. DEAD END

江 郎 才 尽

Pinyin: Jīang Láng cái jìn

Cantonese: Gòng Lòhng chòih jeuhn

江 Jiang (surname)
郎 Lang (diminutive)
才 talent
尽 exhausted

Literal meaning: Jiang Lang's talent is exhausted

Meaning: one lacks inspiration

English equivalent: at the end of one's tether

Story: Jiang Yān (江淹) was a famous literary man in the second half of fifth century. When he was young his poems earned him great fame so everyone called him Master Jiang. In later life his compositions deteriorated, so then people said, "Ah, his talent is used up!"

There are two stories to account for this. According to the first, he dreams he is travelling by boat and a man asks him to give back some silk; he takes the silk from his pocket and returns it, keeping only a few feet for himself. As a result his writings become less and less interesting.

In the other he dreams of a famous literary man asking him to give back his brush; when he returns the brush he has no more beautiful words from which to fashion his poems.

Note: Jiang Yan's essays and poems deteriorated because he changed his lifestyle, thinking he had better enjoy himself while he could. In his later years, he preferred comfort to hard work. So

16

the two stories were either invented by others or used as an excuse by himself. In contrast his contemporary Yǔ Xìn（庾信）improved as he got older because he had a harder life and in his writing drew on his life experience.

Nowadays in Putonghua *Jiang Lang* would be *Xiǎo Jiang*（小江）. In modern Cantonese we use *Gòng Jái*（江仔）as a term of affection or diminutive.

Besides people's surname 'jiang'（江）means river.

Related vocabulary

江河日下 (jiāng hé rì xià) go from bad to worse
牛郎 (niúláng) the cowherd in the legend about the moon
女郎 (nǚláng) young woman
才能 (cáinéng) ability, talent
文才 (wéncái) literary talent
尽心尽力 (jìnxīn jìnlì) with all one's heart and might
穷尽 (qióngjìn) limit, end
无穷无尽 (wúqióng wújìn) boundless, infinite

9. CONTRADICTION

自相矛盾

Pinyin: zì xiāng máo dùn

Cantonese: jih sèung màauh téuhn

自 oneself
相 mutual
矛 spear
盾 shield

Literal meaning: spear and shield negate each other

Meaning: self-contradictory

Story: Once upon a time in China there was a man who sold shields and spears. First he praised the strength of his shields, saying they were so tough no spear could pierce them. Next he praised his spears: these were so sharp they could pierce anything. One of the bystanders suggested he try out one of his spears on one of his shields. The salesman was struck dumb.

Note: This ironical little story is the origin of the expression which describes a group in which the members all hold conflicting views or have conflicting interests. It can be used to described internal conflicts, 'nèibù máodùn' (内部矛盾) or international conflicts 'guójì máodùn' (国际矛盾).

Related vocabulary

自己 (zìjǐ) oneself
自觉 (zìjué) conscious, aware
自修 (zìxiū) self-study
自由 (zìyòu) liberty, free
相对 (xiāngduì) opposite, face to face; relative

相逢 (xiāngféng) meet
相识 (xiāngshǐ) be acquainted with each other
相同 (xiāngtóng) the same

10. NO FREE LUNCH

守 株 待 兔

Pinyin: shǒu zhū dài tù

Cantonese: sáu jyù doih tou

守 keep watch
株 a stump
待 wait for
兔 rabbits

Literal meaning: stand by the stump waiting for more rabbits to come

Meaning: to want something for nothing

Story: One day a farmer saw a rabbit run headlong into a tree stump and drop dead. He took it home and ate it. "This is great," he said to himself. "If I can get a rabbit like this every day, there's no need to work any more." From then on he stopped going to work in his fields and spent all day waiting by the tree stump for another rabbit. He waited and waited, but no rabbit. Meanwhile his fields lay abandoned and the food ran out. The farmer starved.

Note: The foolish farmer wants something for nothing. There is another Chinese saying, 'bù láo ér huò' (不劳而获), reap without sowing. People like this confuse the normal and the accidental. The farmer's job is to farm, and barring acts of God or war, he makes a living at it. It's not too bright to give up work in the hope of a lucky chance.

Note the difference:
待 (dài): 等待 (děngdài) **wait**
侍 (shì): 侍女 (shìnǚ) **maid**

兔 (tù): 兔子 (tùzi) rabbit
免 (miǎn): 免除 (miǎnchú) exempt; avoid

Related vocabulary

守法 (shǒufǎ) law-abiding
守候 (shǒuhòu) to expect, to wait for something
守卫 (shǒuwèi) to guard, defend
待业 (dàiyè) to wait for a job
期待 (qídài) to expect
招待 (zhaōdài) receive guests,
　　entertain, serve customers

11. TRUE FRIENDS

刎 颈 之 交

Pinyin: wěn jǐng zhī jiāo

Cantonese: máhn géng jì gàau

刎 cut

颈 neck

之 of

交 friendship

Literal meaning: friendship of the cutting necks kind

Meaning: true friends, willing to die for each other

English equivalent: Damon and Pythias

Story: This happened during the Warring States Period, when Lìn Xiāngrú（蔺相如）of Zhāo（赵）returned home after accomplishing his mission and saving the *bì*, told in the story 'wén bì guī zhào' "完璧归赵" on page 28. Having done his country such great service, he was prompted to a high position.

General Lían Pō（廉颇）was unhappy about this. He felt it unfair that he who had fought bravely on the battlefield and undergone many dangers should now have a lower rank than Lin, and swore that he would find an opportunity of insulting him. When Lin heard about this he did his best to aviod meeting Lian Po. If he even saw his carriage in the distance he would avoid it. Lin's staff thought they lost face because their master was afraid. Some even resigned. So Lin told them, "The country has me for diplomacy, but for military affairs we need Lian Po. That is why our country is strong and secure and no foreign power will attack us. If we two don't get along, the enemy will take advantage. That would be very bad for the country."

When Lian Po heard this he felt ashamed. He stripped to the waist and came to Lin's home, carrying a big wooden stick. He knelt and begged forgiveness, asking Lin to beat him with the stick. Lin threw away the stick and invited him to sit. They began to talk and became faithful friends.

Note: This story shows the far-sightedness of Lin Xiangru and Lian Po's courage in admitting his mistake. We should not allow personal animosity to damage the general interest.

Another version of the saying is 'fùjīng gǐngzuì' (负荆请罪), proffer a birch and ask for a flogging. 'Fù' (负) means " carry on the back or shoulder " .

Related vocabulary

自刎 (zìwěn) to cut one's throat
交换 (jiāohuàn) exchange
交际 (jiāojì) social intercourse
交情 (jiāoqing) friendship
交涉 (jiāoshè) negotiate
交谈 (jiāotán) talk with each other
交通 (jiāotōng) traffic
交易 (jiāoyì) trade, a business deal
交友 (jiāoyóu) to make friends

12. HOT AIR

纸 上 谈 兵

Pinyin: zhǐ shàng tán bīng

Cantonese: jí seuhng tàahm bìng

纸 paper

上 on

谈 discuss

兵 troops

Literal meaning: to discuss troop movements on paper

Meaning: to be an armchair strategist

English equivalent: talk hot air

Story: During the Warring States Period a general of Zhao had a son, Zhào Kuò （赵括）, who was young but very good at talking about military strategy. Even his father found it impossible to refute him. But his father thought his son could not be a great general. If one day he became one, the country would suffer disasters because he seemed to think moving the army was too easy. Later when Qin invaded Zhao, the king of Zhao sent Lian Po to resist. Lian Po first defended and then waited for an opportunity to attack. The Qin army couldn't advance. So they spread the rumor that Qin only feared Zhao Kuo. So the king replaced Lian Po with Zhao Kuo. Even the chief minister Lin Xiangru and Zhao Kuo's mother tried to change the decision. But he wouldn't listen. So Zhao Kuo became commander and changed Lian Po's strategy. The result was of course a disaster and the whole army of 400,000 was destroyed. Zhao Kuo himself was killed by an arrow.

Note: Zhao Kuo's defeat came about because he only knew theories and had no real practical experience. He did not know that in warfare the time, the place and the people are always changing. In addition he was young and arrogant and had no understanding of personal relations. How could he not fail?

See also 'wěn jǐng zhī jiào' （刎颈之交） on page 22 and 'wán bì guī zhào' （完璧归赵） on page 28.

Related vocabulary

纸板 (zhǐbǎn) cardboard
纸币 (zhǐbì) notes
纸张 (zhǐzhāng) paper
谈话 (tánhuà) conversation
谈论 (tánlùn) to discuss
谈判 (tánpàn) negotiations
兵器 (bīngqì) weapons
士兵 (shìbīng) a soldier

13. SIGN YOUR OWN DEATH WARRANT

作 法 自 毙

Pinyin: zuò fǎ zì bì

Cantonese: jok faat jih baih

作 make
法 law
自 self
毙 kill

Literal meaning: (he who) made the law hurt himself

Meaning: to fall foul of a law of one's own making, to be hoist with one's own petard

English equivalent: to fry in one's own grease

Story: During the Warring States Period Xiào Gōng （孝公）, the King of Qin, wanted his country to be strong so he appointed Shāng Yāng （商鞅） as Prime Minister. Shang Yang made new laws. Though the laws were not exceptionally harsh, within seven years Qin had been transformed into a very powerful state. However the new laws were prejudicial to the interests of a group of nobles and when Xiao Gong died and was succeeded by his son, they accused Shang Yang of treachery. Before the new king came to the throne he was already not very favorably disposed towards Shang Yang, so he immediately ordered his arrest. Shang Yang had no choice but to flee. When he wanted to stay at an inn the innkeeper turned him away because he would not give his name, saying it was against the law to take in travellers without identification. Shang Yang sighed deeply and said to himself: "Little did I think when I set this law that it would fall on my own head." He was arrested and sent back. His punishment was to be pulled apart by five horse-drawn carts, a form of punishment he had also prescribed himself.

Note: This saying is normally used in a negative sense.

'Bì' (毙) and 'sǐ' (死) have the same meaning, but the former is negative, and the later is neutral.

Related vocabulary

作法 (zuòfǎ) way of doing things
作曲 (zuòqǔ) to compose music
制作 (zhìzuò) to manufacture
法官 (fǎguān) a judge
法律 (fǎlǜ) law, statute
法庭 (fǎtíng) a court
自由 (zìyóu) freedom
毙命 (bìmìng) to meet a violent death

14. RESTORE

完 璧 归 赵

Pinyin: wán bì guī Zhào

Cantonese: yùhn bīk gwài Jiuh

完 intact
璧 *bi* (jade)
归 return to
赵 Zhao

bi
(Warring States Period)

Literal meaning: to restore the *bi* intact to Zhao

Meaning: to return something unimpaired to its owner

Story: During the Warring States Period, the state of Zhao owned a piece of precious *bi* which the king of Qin coveted. He sent an envoy to Zhao to tell the king he was willing to exchange fifteen cities for the *bi*. Since Zhao was much weaker than Qin, the king of Zhao could not simply refuse, though he feared the king of Qin intended to cheat him. So he was at a loss what to do. Eventually one of his ministers called Lin Xiangru said he would take the *bi* to Qin. "If Qin is really willing to give the cities in exchange," he said, "I will leave him the *bi*. If not, I will bring it back intact to Zhao."

When Lin gave the *bi* to the king of Qin he realized that the latter had no intention of handing over the cities. So, pretending he wanted to point out some flaw in the stone, he asked for it back. Once it was in his hands he grasped a column, and cried out in great anger, "I see you have no intention of handing over the cities. If you try to take the *bi* by force, I will smash both my own head and the *bi* against this pillar." Fearing that he would do as he said, the king promised to keep his word. Lin asked for a few days' grace to prepare a ceremonial handing over. The king agreed and Lin took the opportunity of having the *bi* secretly taken out of the country. When the day for the exchange arrived, Lin told what he had done. The king of Qin was furious, but for the sake of face and friendly relations between the two countries he let Lin go.

Note: *Bi* is a piece of fine-quality jade in the shape of disc with a round hole in the middle (see photo).

Note the difference:

璧 (bì): jade *bi*
壁 (bì): 墙壁 (qiángbì) wall

Related vocabulary

完备 (wánbèi) perfect
完满 (wánmǎn) successful, satisfactory
完全 (wánquán) whole, complete
完整 (wánzhěng) intact
璧还 (bìhuán) to return a borrowed
　　object, decline a gift
归国 (guīguó) to return to one's country
归家 (guījiā) to return home

15. PARANOID

杯弓蛇影

Pinyin: bēi gōng shé yǐng

Cantonese: bùi gùng sèh yíng

杯　cup

弓　bow

蛇　snake

影　shadow

Literal meaning: the reflection of the bow in the cup looks like a snake

Meaning: unfounded suspicions

English equivalent: take every bush for a bugbear

Story: A man suddenly remembered that a friend who used to drink with him hadn't been to see him for a long while. So he sent to inquire after his friend's health. The friend sent this reply: "Last time I was at your house I discovered a little snake floating in the wine cup. Out of politeness, I drank it. But ever since, I have felt unwell." Puzzled to know what could be the cause of this, the man looked all around his home.

Eventually he spotted a colored bow hanging on the wall and realised what had happened: the reflection of the bow in the wine cup created the appearance of a little snake. He invited his friend to come over and explained it to him.

When the psychological cause was revealed, the friend's illness was cured.

Note: Another similar saying is 'yóngrén zì rǎo' （庸人自扰）, stupid people worry themselves for nothing.

Related vocabulary

杯子 (bēizi) cup, glass
酒杯 (jiǔbēi) wine glass
弓箭 (gōngjiàn) bow and arrow
弓形 (gōngxíng) bow-shaped, curved
影子 (yǐngzi) shadow, reflection
电影 (diànyǐng) movie
电影院 (diànyǐngyuàn) cinema

16. PIG HEADED

刻 舟 求 剑

Pinyin: kè zhōu qiú jiàn

Cantonese: hāk jàu kàuh gim

刻 mark

舟 the boat

求 find

剑 the sword

Literal meaning: marking the boat to find the sword

Meaning: to take measures without regard to changing circumstances

Story: Once upon a time a man who was crossing the river by boat accidentally dropped his sword. Unperturbed, he made a mark on the side of the boat and said, "This is where the sword fell in." When they reached the other side, he used the mark to look for the sword, but naturally he couldn't find it.

Note: Rivers have always been regarded as symbols of change and passing time. The world is indeed like a river, ever changing, ever moving on. So if you try to hold onto just one method of doing things all your life, it won't work.

Related vocabulary

刻薄 (kèbó) unkind

刻意 (kèyì) painstakingly

雕刻 (diāokè) to carve

时刻 (shíkè) time, moment

求婚 (qiúhūn) to make an offer of marriage

求学 (qiúxué) to attend school; seek knowledge

请求 (qǐngqiú) to ask, request
要求 (yāoqiú) to demand, require
剑术 (jiànshù) fencing

17. NARROW ESCAPE

图 穷 匕 现

Pinyin: tú qióng bǐ xiàn

Cantonese: tòuh kùhng bei yihn

图 map

穷 end

匕 dagger

现 appear

Literal meaning: when the map is unrolled the dagger appears

Meaning: the plot is revealed in the end

Story: In the last years of the Warring States Period, the state of Qin was very strong and had taken over many other states. In the north-east there was a state called Yān（燕）, whose prince wanted to save his country from being invaded by Qin. He sent Qín Kē（荆轲）and an assistant to assassinate the king of Qin (who later became Qin Shihuang, the first ruler of a united China). They carried a map showing the land which Yan prepared to cede to Qin and the head of a Qin general who had fled to Yan. Qin Ke went in front carrying the head in a box and his assistant followed with the map. They were received by the king of Qin in his palace.

As they mounted the steps to the palace, the assistant was suddenly seized with fear and trembling. Realizing that the king was becoming suspicious, Qin Ke quickly gave him the box and took the map from his assistant. When the map began to unroll the dagger hidden in it was revealed. Qin Ke grasped the dagger in one hand and seized the king's sleeve with the other. He wanted to force the king to promise to return all the territories he had taken from other states. The terrified king managed to escape from his grasp, tearing off his sleeve in the process. Qin Ke threw the dragger at him but missed, and was killed on the spot by the king's guards.

Note: This saying is used in a negative sense. It refers to some illegal activity or scheme which is exposed at the last minute.

'Qióng'（穷）more commonly used to mean "poor", it's opposite is 'fù'（富）"rich".

Related vocabulary

图案 (tú'àn) pattern, design
图书馆 (túshūguǎn) library
地图 (dìtú) map
穷尽 (qióngjìn) limit, end
穷苦 (qióngkú) impoverished
穷人 (qióngrén) the poor
贫穷 (pínqióng) poor
匕首 (bǐshǒu) dagger

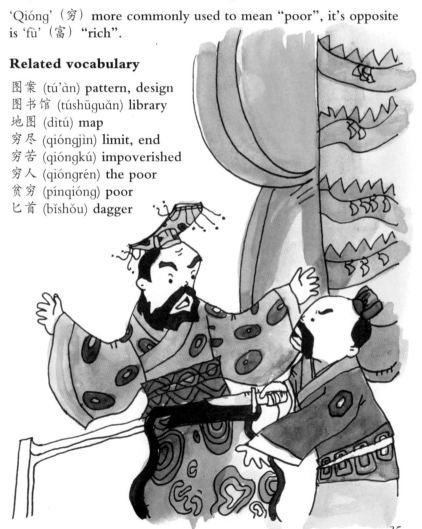

18. GILD THE LILY

画蛇添足

Pinyin: huà shé tiān zú

Cantonese: waahk sèh tìm jūk

画 draw
蛇 snake
添 add
足 feet

Literal meaning: to draw a snake and add legs

Meaning: to overdo something

English equivalent: paint the lily

Story: Some friends were drinking together. They had only one jar of wine and there wasn't enough to go around. So one of them suggested that they all drew a snake; whoever finished first and produced the best likeness should have the wine. Everybody agreed. One of them finished very quickly. He could have claimed the wine, but looking round, he saw that everyone else was still drawing, so he decided he had better do a bit more. So he added legs. The next one to finish looked at the first man's drawing and said, "But snakes don't have legs", and drank the wine.

Note: Adding legs to the drawing of a snake is obviously quite superfluous.

In Putonghua "huà" is both verb and noun, but in Cantonese pronunciation the words are different: the verb is "waahk" and the noun is "wá".

'Zú' (足) in the meaning of "feet", the synonym is 'jiǎo' (脚).

'Jiao' is commonly used in daily life. 'Zu' can mean both "feet" and "enough".

Notice that "tiān" is written 添 not 添

Related vocabulary

画册 (huàcè) a picture album
画稿 (huàgǎo) a sketch
画画 (huàhuà) to paint a picture
增添 (zēngtiān) to add, increase
充足 (chōngzú) sufficient, abundant
满足 (mǎnzú) satisfied, contented

19. WHEELS WITHIN WHEELS

歧 路 亡 羊

Pinyin: qí lù wáng yáng

Cantonese: kèih louh mòhng yèuhng

歧 forked

路 road

亡 stray

羊 sheep

Literal meaning: a sheep straying in a forked road

Meaning: one cannot find the truth if one sets off in the wrong direction

English equivalent: there are wheels within wheels

Story: Yáng Zhū (杨朱) was a famous thinker who lived in the Warring States Period. One day his neighbor lost a sheep. He and his family went out looking for it and he asked all his relatives to come and look for it too. "Why trouble so many people for the sake of a single sheep?" Yang Zhu asked. The neighbor replied: "The road has many forks so we need more people to search." In the end everyone came back empty-handed. Yang Zhu asked again, "How could you not find the sheep, when so many of you went out to look?" They answered: "Every forked road forked again, so we couldn't find it." When Yang zhu heard this he sat there gloomily ruminating. His student asked him why. He sighed and said, "The road keeps branching. When a sheep is lost, it cannot be easily found. The same applies to us scholars: if we don't have a correct method to learn, we will never achieve anything."

Note: "Yang" is a surname, "Zhu" is a given name. Also call Yángzǐ（杨子）. 'Zi'（子）was an ancient title of respect for a learned or virtuous man. Yangzi means "Master Yang".

Do not confuse the following:

亡 (wáng): loss, lose; death
忘 (wáng): can't remember
忙 (máng): busy, no free time
芒 (máng): awn

Related vocabulary

路标 (lùbiāo) road sign
路途 (lùtú) path, way
路障 (lùzhàng) roadblock
出路 (chūlù) way out
死亡 (sǐwáng) death
羊毛 (yángmáo) wool
羊群 (yángqún) a flock of sheep
羊肉 (yángròu) mutton

20. ILLUSION

南 柯 一 梦

Pinyin: Nán Kē yī mèng

Cantonese: Nàahm Ò yāt muhng

南 south

柯 branch

一 one

梦 dream

Literal meaning: a dream of the southern branch

Meaning: an empty dream, illusion

Story: A gentleman of the Táng Dynasty was celebrating his birthday party under a big tree. He became quite drunk so he went back inside and lay down in the corridor. Hazily he saw two men in purple approach. They invited him to mount a carriage with them and then drove him straight towards the tree. Passing into a great cave he arrived at an earthly paradise named Huái Ān Guó（槐安国）, where the king gave him his daughter in marriage and made him governor of Nánkē（南柯）province. He governed there twenty years, enjoying great wealth and honor. He governed well and led the army to victory.

Later the princess died of an illness and he became so unhappy that the king advised him to return home. He bade farewell with tears in his eyes and rode out of the cave on a simple horse wagon. He came to his own house which looked exactly as it had been twenty years before. When he got down from the wagon, he saw himself lying in the corridor. He then awoke and was astonished to see the servants were still clearing the cups and plates from the party. In an instant of time he had dreamed the passing of twenty years. He and his friends went to look at the big tree and found a big ants' nest under the tree. So that was the cave he went into. Huai An Guo was nothing but an ant hill!

Note: A similar saying is 'huáng liáng yī mèng' (黄粱一梦), a golden millet dream. In this story, a sad and disenchanted scholar staying at a small inn meets a Taoist priest who gives him a porcelain pillow. The inkeeper is cooking millet for dinner. When he sleeps on the pillow, he dreams of passing the civil service exam and enjoying great wealth and success. When he awakes and finds it was only a dream, the innkeeper's millet is not yet cooked.

Related vocabulary

南针 (nánzhēn) a guide (to action)
梦境 (mèngjìng) dreamland
梦想 (mèngxiǎng) to dream of, vainly hope
做梦 (zuòmèng) to dream
夜长梦多 (yècháng mèngduō) a long night is filled with dreams — a long delay means many problems

21. LIAR

指 鹿 为 马

Pinyin: zhǐ lù wéi mǎ

Cantonese: jí luhk wàih máh

指　point at
鹿　deer
为　call it
马　a horse

Literal meaning: to point at a deer and call it a horse

Meaning: to distort the facts; to call black white

Story: Qin Shihuang after uniting the kingdom in 221 BC, reigned for twelve years. At his death, he was succeeded by his son, Hú Hài（胡亥）, who was known as Èrshì（二世）, the second. Ershi was incompetent and all the power fell into the hands of his chief minister Zhào Gāo（赵高）, who had ambitions to be emperor himself. Zhao Gao wanted to test the ministers' feelings towards himself. One day he brought a deer which he presented to Ershi, telling him that it was a horse. Ershi wasn't sure about this, so he asked the ministers, "Is it a stag or a horse?" The ministers were afraid of Zhao Gao and most of them didn't dare speak out. Some kept silent and others, to please Zhao Gao, affirmed that it was a horse. Only a few said it was a stag. Afterwards Zhao Gao framed charges against all those who had said it was a stag. A few months later he engineered Ershi's death.

Note: This saying is only used negatively.

A similar saying is 'diāndǎo hēibái'（颠倒黑白）to reverse black and white.

Note the difference:

指 (zhǐ): 手指 (shǒuzhǐ) a finger
趾 (zhǐ): 脚趾 (jiǎozhǐ) toenail

Related vocabulary

指甲 (zhǐjiǎ) fingernail
指示 (zhǐshì) to indicate, to instruct
为非作歹 (wéi fēi zuò dǎi) to do evil,
    commit crime
为止 (wéizhǐ) up to, till
行为 (xíngwéi) action, behaviour

22. TOUGH TRAINING

卧薪尝胆

Pinyin: wò xīn cháng dǎn

Cantonese: ngoh sàn sèuhng dáam

卧 sleep

薪 firewood

尝 taste

胆 gall bladder

Literal meaning: to sleep on firewood and taste gall bladder

Meaning: to toughen oneself up for some great task

Story: During the Spring and Autumn Period the King of Wú (吴) led his army against Yuè (越), was seriously wounded and died. His son Fú Chāi (夫差) succeeded him. Three years later Fu Chai defeated Yue and their king, Gōu Jiàn (勾践), was captured and taken to Wu. While he was in captivity, he did all he could to please Fu Chai and get his trust. Eventually Fu Chai let him return home. After returning to his own country, Gou Jian wanted to build up his strength. Every night he slept on firewood and he also kept some gall bladder by his bed. Before eating and sleeping, he insisted on tasting the gall bladder. After a long period of preparation he eventually defeated Wu.

Note: Nowadays the word 'xīn' (薪) is used in 'xīnjīng' (薪金) or 'xīnshuǐ' (薪水) meaning salary, since in modern times a salary is as essential to life as fire and water once were.

Newspaper job advertisements often refer to 'gāoxīn' (高薪) — high salary.

Note the difference:

胆 (dǎn): 胆敢 (dǎngǎn) **to dare**
担 (dān): 担任 (dānrèn) **to hold a post, assume an office**

Related vocabulary

卧病 (wòbìng) **to be confined to bed**
卧室 (wòshì) **a bedroom**
年薪 (niánxīn) **yearly salary**
月薪 (yuèxīn) **monthly salary**
尝试 (chángshì) **to try**
胆大 (dǎndà) **bold, audacious**
胆识 (dǎnshí) **courage and insight**
胆小 (dǎnxiǎo) **timid, cowardly**

23. TRAPPED

请君入瓮

Pinyin: qǐng jūn rù wèng

Cantonese: chíng gwàn yahp ung

请 please
君 you
入 enter
瓮 vat

Literal meaning: kindly step into the vat

Meaning: to be caught by your own scheme, hoist with your own petard

Story: During the time of Wǔ Zétiān (武则天), the famous Chinese empress (684–704), someone reported that Zhóu Xīng (周兴) was plotting against the state. The Empress sent Lái Jùn chén (来俊臣) to investigate. Lai Junchen invited Zhou Xing to his house. During the banquet he asked Zhou Xing what was the best way to force prisoners to admit their crimes. "Easy," said Zhou Xing. "Just get a large vat and heat it with firewood all around, then order the prisoners to get in. They will confess anything and everything." Lai Junchen said, "That's a good idea," and ordered that a vat be prepared immediately. Turning to Zhou Xing he said, "I have received orders from the Empress to put you on trial, so please confess or step into the vat." The terrified Zhou kowtowed and pleaded guilty.

Note: In this saying "jūn" means "you", as in the popular song, 'hé rì jūn zài lái' (何日君再来), "when are you coming back?"

It also has three more meanings:
1. After a surname as a respectful title: 'chén jūn' (陈君)

2. In ancient China it was used for the head of state 'guójūn' （国君）. The opposite was 'chén' （臣）subject.
3. It was also once used between husband and wife.

Related vocabulary

请愿 (qǐngyuàn) to petition
聘请 (pìnqǐng) to engage
申请 (shēngqǐng) to apply for something
君主 (jūnzhǔ) a monarch
君子 (jūnzi) a gentleman
入场 (rùchǎng) admission
入口 (rùkǒu) entrance

24. CONNIVE

狼 狈 为 奸

Pinyin: láng bèi wéi jiān

Cantonese: lòhng buì wàih gàan

狼 wolf

狈 wolf

为 together

奸 evil

Literal meaning: two kinds of wolf combine to do ill

Meaning: to act together, to be in cahoots

English equivalent: play into each other's hands

Story: The *bei* was a legendary animal like a wolf with very short front legs, which tends to put its front legs on the back of a wolf. This works particularly well because the wolf is supposed to have shorter back legs. Without the *bei*, the wolf can't stand; with the wolf the *bei* can't walk. So *lang* (wolf) and *bei* always combine to attack other animals. If they want to attack a sheep pen the wolf can ride on the *bei*'s shoulder while the *bei* stands on his long back legs. The wolf will use his two long front legs to pull the sheep out.

Note: The opposite of 'jiān' (奸) is 'zhōng' (忠), loyal, and a saying which has similar meaning is 'péng bǐ wéi jiān' (朋比为奸), to conspire or act in collusion with.

Note the difference:

狼 (láng) **a wolf**

狠 (hěn) **ruthless**

Related vocabulary

奸细 (jiānxi) **a spy**
奸邪 (jiānxié) **crafty**
奸淫 (jiānyín) **adultery**
奸诈 (jiānzhà) **treacherous, crafty**

25. NO RETREAT

破 釜 沉 舟

Pinyin: pò fǔ chén zhōu

Cantonese: po fú chàhn jàu

破 break

釜 cauldron

沉 sink

舟 boat

Literal meaning: to break the cauldrons and sink the boats

Meaning: cut off all means of retreat

English equivalent: go for broke, burn one's bridges

Story: At the beginning of the second century BC, after the kingdom established by Qin Shihuang had been broken up, anarchy reigned. Many leaders rose up against the Qin state. One of these, General Xiàng Yǔ（项羽）of Chǔ（楚）, led a great army against Qin. Obliged to cross a river, he ordered his troops afterwards to sink all the boats, break the cooking vessels, burn down the tents and carry with them food for three days only. The aim of this was to strengthen their resolve to fight to the end and never retreat. After a fierce battle, the army Qin was defeated and Xiang Yu became supreme.

Note: A similar saying is 'qū zhù yī zhì'（孤注一掷）stake everything on a single throw. 'Pò fǔ chén zhōu' has positive sense and 'qū zhù yī zhì', the negative.

Note the difference:

釜 (fǔ): 铁釜 (tiěfǔ) an ancient Chinese cooking vessel, a cauldron

斧 (fǔ): 斧头 (fǔtou) an axe

Related vocabulary

破坏 (pòhuài) to destroy
破旧立新 (pò jiù lì xīn) to destroy the old and establish the new
破烂 (pòlàn) ragged, tattered
沉迷 (chénmí) indulge
沉没 (chénmò) sink
沉默 (chénmò) reticent; silent
沉痛 (chéntòng) deep feeding of grief, deeply felt
沉重 (chénzhòng) serious; heavy
沉住气 (chénzhuqì) keep calm
沉醉 (chénzuì) become intoxicated

26. ONCE BITTEN TWICE SHY

惊弓之鸟

Pinyin: jīng gōng zhī niǎo

Cantonese: gìng gùng jì níuh

惊 startle

弓 bow

之 of

鸟 bird

Literal meaning: a bird startled by the bow

Meaning: very frightened

English equivalent: once bitten twice shy

Story: In ancient China there was a general who was an expert archer. Once when he was out hunting with the king he heard the cry of a goose close at hand. Looking up, he saw a goose flying over head. He turned to the king and said: "Watch this. I can bring that bird down without even using an arrow." He twanged his bowstring and the bird fell. The king asked him to explain. "It's not my archery, it's the goose itself which had a problem. I could see he was flying more slowly than normal, so he must already be weak or wounded. The sound of my bowstring gave him such a scare that he fell."

Note: In this story the archer was also something of a detective. Just from the cry and appearance of the goose he deduced that something was wrong with it.

This saying is pejorative. Its connotation is close to that of 'lòu wǎng zhī yú' (漏网之鱼), which generally means "a fugitive criminal or defeated enemies who have escaped".

Related vocabulary

惊人 (jīngrén) astonishing
惊喜 (jīngxǐ) pleasantly surprised
惊醒 (jīngxǐng) awaken, rouse suddenly from sleep
鸟瞰 (niǎkàn) get a bird's-eye view; general survey of a subject

27. PSYCHOLOGY

望 梅 止 渴

Pinyin: wàng méi zhǐ kě

Cantonese: mohng mùih jí hot

望 watch

梅 plum

止 stop

渴 thirst

Literal meaning: to quench your thirst by looking at plums

Meaning: to overcome some problem using psychology and one's imagination

Story: During the Three Kingdoms Period, the famous general Cáo Cáo（曹操）was leading his army to a distant battle front. The weather was exceedingly hot and the soldiers were thirsty, there was no water and everybody was grumbling. Cao Cao's solution was to pick up his whip and point in front: "There is a large grove of plumtrees ahead," he told them. "They are sweet, those plums, and sour as well. They will certainly quench your thirst." His words made the soldiers imagine the taste of plums in their mouths. Their mouths began to water and they forgot their thirst. They went forward peaceably till they reached a well.

Note: A similar saying is 'hùa bǐng cōng jī'（画饼充饥）, draw a cake to stop hunger.

Do not confuse 'kě'（渴）and 'hē'（喝）,

口渴 (kǒukě) thirsty
喝水 (hēshuǐ) to drink water

In Cantonese, both are pronounced the same, "hot".

Related vocabulary

渴望 (kěwàng) to long for
希望 (xīwàng) to hope, wish, expect
愿望 (yuànwàng) to desire, aspiration
禁止吸烟 (jìnzhǐ xīyān) No Smoking
停止 (tíngzhǐ) to stop

28. HIT THE BOOKS

悬 梁 刺 股

Pinyin: xuán liáng cì gǔ

Cantonese: yùhn lèuhng chi gú

悬 hang
梁 beam
刺 prick
股 thigh

Literal meaning: to hang from a beam and prick one's thigh

Meaning: to study very hard

Story: There are two stories here, both concerning the Warring States Period.

The first is of a student called Sūn Jìng （孙敬）who studied morning and night. In the middle of night when he was really tired he tied himself by the hair to a beam to prevent himself from nodding off. Later he became a famous scholar.

In the second, Sū Qín （苏秦）was a strategist who tried to persuade the king of Qin to unite China. His advice was rejected so he returned home a failure to the displeasure of his family. Undeterred, he set himself to study hard; when he was tired and felt sleepy he would pick up an awl and jab himself in the thigh till the blood flowed. Later he persuaded the six warring states to unite against Qin and became chief minister of the confederation.

Related vocabulary

悬挂 (xuánguà) to hang
悬殊 (xuánshū) a wide gap, disparity

刺激 (cìjī) to stimulate, provoke
刺绣 (cìxiù) to embroider
行刺 (xíngcì) to assassinate
股东 (gǔdōng) a shareholder
股份 (gǔfèn) share, stock
股票 (gǔpiào) share certificate
股息 (gǔxì) dividend

29. DETERMINATION

愚公移山

Pinyin: yú gōng yí shān

Cantonese: yùh gùng yìh sàan

愚 foolish
公 old man
移 move
山 mountain

Literal meaning: the foolish old man moved the mountain

Meaning: to succeed through determination

Story: There was once an old man of nearly ninety. In front of his house were two big mountains blocking the way. When they wanted to go somewhere they had to go round them. It was very inconvenient. The old man held a family meeting and suggested they all get together to move the two mountains. Everyone agreed. So the old man, his son and his grandson started digging. A wise old man called Zhì Sóu (智叟) admonished them: "You are wasting your energy. You are old and there are so few of you, how can you possibly succeed? Why not just relax and enjoy your old age?" But the old man replied, "Although I myself won't live much longer, when I die my son will continue and my son's sons, and so on forever. The mountain will not keep growing, so one day inevitably it will be flattened." Zhi Sou had no answer to this. The God of Earth also heard about it and reported the story to the God of Heaven, who was so moved by the old man's fortitude that he sent two powerful spirits to carry the two mountains away.

Note: For centuries this fable helps to shape the Chinese national character in its steadfastness and perseverance, especially in the agrarian society.

A modern revival of this praise-worthy spirit generated afresh an impetus by bringing it to a new moral apex.

'Gōng' (公) can also mean public as in 'gōngyòng' (公用), for public use. The opposite is 'sī' (私).

Related vocabulary

愚笨 (yúbèn) foolish, stupid, clumsy
愚蠢 (yúchún) stupid, foolish
愚弄 (yúnòng) make a fool of
移动 (yídòng) move, shift
移民 (yímín) migrate
移山倒海 (yíshān dǎohǎi) remove
   mountain and drain seas —
   transform nature

30. IMPATIENCE

揠 苗 助 长

Pinyin: yà miáo zhù zhǎng

Cantonese: aat mìuh joh jéung

揠 pull
苗 shoots
助 help
长 grow

Literal meaning: pull the shoots to help them to grow

Meaning: to spoil something through impatience

Story: A farmer once was worried about his rice shoots because they weren't growing fast enough. So one by one he pulled them so that they all looked taller. When he went home he said to his son: "I'm exhausted, but all my shoots have grown." The son couldn't understand, so he rushed to the field to look. All the shoots had withered.

Note: 'Yà' (揠) is no longer used, so you will also see this saying with the modern equivalent 'bá' (拔).

"长" also pronounced as "cháng". Please see "Related vocabulary".

Note the difference:
苗 (miáo): 幼苗 (yòumiáo) seedling
笛 (dí): 汽笛 (qìdí) steam whistle

Related vocabulary

苗床 (miáochuáng) seedbed
苗圃 (miáopǔ) a nursery (for plants)

苗条 (miáotiao) slim, slender (of a woman)
帮助 (bāngzhù) to help
补助 (bǔzhù) a subsidy, an allowance
长处 (chángchu) good qualities, good point
长久 (chángjiǔ) for a long time
长大 (zhǎngdà) to grow up
长者 (zhǎngzhě) senior
生长 (shēngzhǎng) grow; to be brought up
市长 (shìzhǎng) mayor

31. CHARLATAN

滥竽充数

Pinyin: làn yú chōng shù

Cantonese: láahm yùh chùng sou

滥 **extra**

竽 *yu,* **an instrument**

充 **make up**

数 **number**

Literal meaning: pass oneself off as a player to make up the number

Meaning: to be there just to make up the number, to perform no useful service

Story: In ancient China there was a king who loved to hear the *yu* (竽), an ancient wind instrument. He liked to have an ensemble of three hundred people playing together. One scholar who couldn't play at all pretended to be an expert and asked to join the ensemble. The king was delighted and paid him a high fee. When the king died, his son who succeeded him also loved the *yu,* but he preferred to hear it on its own. When he asked each of the players to perform a solo, the charlatan ran away.

Note: This saying can be used of oneself for the sake of modesty.

Note the difference:

竽 (yú): 吹竽 (chuī yú) to blow *yu*

竿 (gān): 竹竿 (zhúgān) bamboo pole

芋 (yù): 芋头 (yùtou) taro

yu

Related vocabulary

滥用 (lànyòng) **abuse**
泛滥 (fànlàn) **be in flood**
充分 (chōngfèn) **abundant**
充足 (chōngzú) **sufficient**
冒充 (màochōng) **to pretend to be**
数量 (shùliàng) **quantity**
数目 (shùmù) **number, amount**

32. BLESSING IN DISGUISE

塞 翁 失 马

Pinyin: Sài wēng shī mǎ

Cantonese: Choi yùng sāt máh

塞　frontier

翁　old man

失　lose

马　horse

Literal meaning: Saiweng lost his horse

Meaning: temporary loss may turn out to be a gain

English equivalent: a blessing in disguise

Story: On the northern frontier there was an old man whom everyone called Sàiwēng（塞翁）. One day he lost a horse. The neighbors all came to comfort him. Actually he didn't mind because he thought losing a horse may bring him some blessing in return. After a few days the lost horse did indeed return with another horse. The neighbors came again to congratulate him. Saiweng wasn't especially pleased. He only said, "I hope this horse will not bring trouble."

Before long Saiweng's son, who was very fond of riding, tried the new horse and fell off and broke his leg. Again people came to comfort the old man and he was not particularly sad; he just said, "My son has broken his leg. Maybe it is a blessing in disguise." Later foreign troops invaded and all the young men in the village had to go to fight. Many were killed. Saiweng's son did not go with them because he was disabled. It saved his life.

Note: Life is indeed always changeable and misfortunes may be blessings in disguise, so this story teaches us to accept misfortune patiently. This in itself will not change our fortunes but it will at least lessen the pain of misfortune. Likewise, if we have some piece of good fortune, we should not be too pleased.

This saying sometimes is used in pair followed by 'yān zhī fēi fú' (焉知非福) who could know that it was not a blessing?

"塞" also pronounced as "sè" as in 'fūyan sèzé' (敷衍塞责) perform one's duty in a perfunctory manner.

Related vocabulary

塞外 (sàiwài) beyond the Great Wall
老渔翁 (lǎo yúwēng) an old fisherman
失败 (shībài) be defeated
失手 (shīshǒu) accidentally drop
失业 (shīyè) be out of work
损失 (sǔnshī) lose
遗失 (yíshī) lose

33. PRACTICE MAKES PERFECT

熟 能 生 巧

Pinyin: shú néng shēng qiǎo

Cantonese: suhk nàhng sàng háau

熟 experience

能 can

生 produce

巧 skill

copper coin
Tang Dynesty

Literal meaning: skill comes from practice

Meaning: practice makes perfect

Story: There was once an expert archer, whose arrows never missed. Everyone greatly admired his skill. One day he gave a show. The audience applauded. But one old man selling oil did not seem particularly impressed. "That is merely skill," the old man said. "What's so special about it?" The archer was angry. He asked the old man to have a go himself. "I am no archer," the latter replied. "But I can show you how to pour oil." He produced a gourd, placed a copper coin over the opening, and using a ladle began to pour oil into it through the hole in the middle of the coin. He poured a lot of oil, but it never even touched the coin. Afterwards he showed everyone the coin: it was completely free of oil. People were amazed and the archer had nothing to say.

Note: This story is quite negative: the oil vendor seems to be saying to the archer, "No big deal, no reason to be so proud of your skill". But the idiom is used in much the same way as the English one, to encourage people.

'Shǔ' (熟) is often used to mean ripe or cooked: 'guāshú dìluò' (瓜

66

熟蒂落), when fruit is ripe it falls; 'fànshú' (饭熟), the rice is cooked.

Related vocabulary

熟路 (shúlù) a familiar route
熟人 (shúrén) an acquaintance
熟食 (shúshí) cooked food
熟睡 (shúshuì) be fast asleep
熟习 (shúxí) to be skilled at
能干 (nénggàn) able, capable
能力 (nénglì) ability
才能 (cáinéng) talent
巧妙 (qiǎomiào) ingenious, clever

34. OPPORTUNIST

鷸蚌相爭，漁人得利

Pinyin: yù bàng xiāng zhēng,
　　　　yú rén dé lì

Cantonese: leuht póhng seùng jàng,
　　　　　yùh yàhn dāk leih

鷸	snipe	漁 ⎫	
蚌	clam	人 ⎬	fisherman
相	mutual	得	gain
爭	fight	利	benefit

Literal meaning: when the snipe and the clam fight, the fisherman benefits

Meaning: it's the third party that benefits from the tussle

English equivalent: two dogs fight for a bone, and a third runs away with it

Story: During the Warring States Period, the king of Zhao was planning a campaign against a neighboring state. A counsellor who disapproved of the idea told him this story. "Down on the shore I saw a snipe attacking a clam. The clam responded by clamping its shell over the snipe's beak. 'Unless it rains today, you're going to be dead,' the snipe said. 'If you can't get your beak free, you'll be dead,' the clam replied. Neither would give way, so in the end a fisherman came along and caught them both. Now, Your Highness' plan to attack our neighbors may produce the same result. If the conflict continues, with neither side winning an outright victory, the state of Qin may play the part of the fisherman." The King of Zhao saw the point and abandoned his plans.

Note: Fish（鱼）and fishing（渔）have the same pronunciation.

渔 (yú): 渔民 (yúmín) fishermen
鱼 (yú): 鱼干 (yúgān) dry fish

Related vocabulary

相比 (xiāngbǐ) compare
相称 (xiāngchèn) to match, suit
相等 (xiāngděng) be equal
相信 (xiāngxīn) believe
获得 (huòdé) to gain, obtain
利息 (lìxī) interest
利用 (lìyàng) make use of
便利 (biànlì) convenient; facilitate

35. MIND YOUR BACK

螳螂捕蝉，黄雀在后

Pinyin: táng láng bǔ chǎn,
huáng què zài hòu

Cantonese: tòhng lòhng bouh sìhm,
wòhng jeuk joih hauh

螳 螂	praying mantis	黄 雀	oriole
捕	catch	在	is
蝉	cicada	后	behind

Literal meaning: the praying mantis stalks the cicada, but the oriole is behind it

Meaning: to be blind to one's own danger

Story: During the Warring States Period, the king of Wu was bent on undertaking a military adventure which his ministers disapproved of. But they did not dare say so. One young man however found a way to voice their objections indirectly. He equipped himself with a bow and arrow and went to the king's garden early in the morning. For three days he roamed in the garden like this and each time his clothes became soaked. Eventually the king called him in and asked what he thought he was doing.

"There is a cicada up there on the tree," the young man said. "It is singing away, but it has no idea a praying mantis is preparing to seize it. And the praying mantis has no idea that an oriole is behind it, poised to strike. And the oriole has no idea that I have it in my sights. These three creatures are all so intent on what they are doing they cannot see the imminent danger." The king saw the point at once and gave up his military adventure.

Related vocabulary

捕捉 (bǔzhuō) catch, seize
逮捕 (dàibǔ) arrest
实在 (shízài) in reality
现在 (xiànzài) now
后悔 (hòuhuǐ) regret
后来 (hòulái) later, afterwards
落后 (luòhòu) to fall behind, to lag

Appendix 1
Hanyu Pinyin System

Each syllable of Hanyu Pinyin is composed of three elements:
1. Initial: the beginning sound element of a syllable.
2. Final: the ending sound element of a syllable or a vowel.
3. Tone: the relative pitch, or variation of pitch, of a syllable.

An example of a syllable:

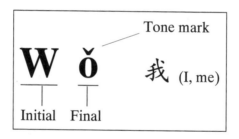

Initials

Group	Pinyin	Yale	*Approximation in English*	*Example*
1	b	b	<u>b</u>ay	bèi 背
	p	p	<u>p</u>ay	pèi 配
	m	m	<u>m</u>ay	mā 妈
	f	f	<u>f</u>ee	fàn 饭
	d	d	<u>d</u>ear	dé 得

	t	t	<u>t</u>ear	tè 特
	n	n	<u>n</u>ear	niǎo 鸟
	l	l	<u>l</u>ean	lín 林
	g	g	<u>g</u>irl	gàn 干
	k	k	<u>k</u>een	kàn 看
	h	h	<u>h</u>eigh	hē 喝
2*	j	j	<u>g</u>ee**	jī 机
	q	ch	<u>ch</u>eese**	qī 七
	x	s	<u>sh</u>e**	xī 西
3*	z	dz	dad'<u>s</u>	zì 自
	c	ts	cat'<u>s</u>	cì 刺
	s	s	<u>s</u>ay	sì 四
	zh	j	<u>j</u>ar	zhī 知
	ch	ch	<u>ch</u>air	chī 吃
	sh	sh	<u>sh</u>ow	shī 诗
	r	r	measu<u>r</u>e	rì 日

* Initials in groups 2 are always followed by finals starting with i or ü while initials in group 3 never precedes finals starting with i or ü.

** To make the j, q and x sound, try to pronounce <u>g</u>ee, <u>ch</u>eese and <u>sh</u>e with the tip of your tongue pressing the ridge (root) of your lower teeth.

Finals

	Pinyin	*Yale*	*Example*
	a	a	sā 撒
	o	o	fó 佛
	e	e	sè 色

	-i		sì 四
	ai	ai	sài 塞
	ei	ei	lèi 累
	ao	au	lǎo 老
	ou	ou	lòu 漏
	an	an	lán 兰
	en	en	rén 人
	ang	ang	ràng 让
	eng	eng	réng 仍
	ong	ung	róng 容
Finals starting with i	i	i	jī 机
	ia	ya	jiā 加
	ie	ye	jiē 接
	iao	yau	jiāo 交
	iou (iu)	you	qiū 秋
	ian	yan	giān 千
	in	in	qīn 亲
	iang	iang	xiǎng 香
	ing	ing	xīng 星
	iong	iung	xiōng 凶
Finals starting with u	u	u	zhū 猪
	ua	wa	zhuā 抓
	uo	wo	zhuō 捉
	uai	wai	shuāi 摔
	uei (ui)	wei	chuī 吹
	uan	wan	chuān 穿
	uen (un)	wun	sūn 孙
	uang	wang	chuāng 窗
	ueng	weng	wēng 翁

Finals	ü	yu	jū 居
starting	üe	ywe	nüè 虐
with	üan	ywan	xuān 宣
ü*	ün	yun	xùn 训

* the two dots can be omitted when a "ü" is preceded by j, q or x.

Tones

Tones	*Symbol*	*Description*	*Example*
1st tone	–	high level	mā 妈
2nd tone	´	rising	má 麻
3rd tone	ˇ	low*	mǎ 马
4th tone	ˋ	falling	mà 罵

* 1. 3rd tone by itself or at the end of a phrase may carry a rising ending.

   2. 3rd tone must change to 2nd tone when it precedes another syllable with 3rd tone.

Apart from the four tones, there is a neutral tone in short, middle pitch is pronounced quickly with no emphasis, as in 'Nǐ hǎo ma?' （你好吗？） "How are you?".

Appendix 2
Cantonese Romanization System

Each syllable of Cantonese is composed of three elements:
1. Initial: the beginning sound element of a syllable.
2. Final: the ending sound element of a syllable or a vowel.
3. Tone: the relative pitch, or variation of pitch, of a syllable.

An example of a syllable:

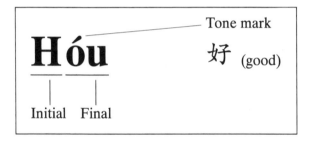

Another example of a syllable:

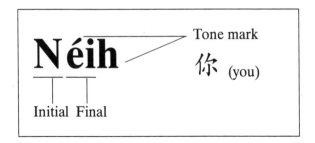

Initials

	as in English	*example*
B	boy	ba
P	park	pa
D	dig	da
T	till	ta
G	game	ga
K	kill	ka
F	far	fa
H	home	ha
N	no	na
L	law	la
J	Jesus	ja
Ch	cheque	cha
M	mother	ma
Ng	singer	nga
Gw	language	gwa
Kw	quite	kwa
S	sand	sa
W	water	wa
Y	yes	ya

Finals

AA		
	as in English	*example*
a	father	chà 叉
aai	aisle	tàai 呔

aau	owl	bàau 飽
aam	arm	sàam 衫
aan	aunt	sàan 山
aang	crown	sàang 生
aak	ark (tongue not curled)	baak 百
aap	harp ("p" mute) (tongue not curled)	daap 答
aat	art ("k" mute) (tongue not curled)	baat 八

A		
ai	sigh	sai 细
au	out ("t" mute)	sàu 收
am	sum	gàm 金
an	sun	fàn 分
ang	dung	gāng 羹
ak	duck ("k" mute)	dāk 得
ap	up ("p" mute)	jāp 汁
at	but	māt 乜

E		
e	yes	jè 遮
ek	echo	sek 钖
eng	length	tèng 听
eu	her (tongue not curled)	hèu 靴
euk	turk ("k" mute) (tongue not curled)	jeuk 着
eung	(l)ear(ni)ng	hèung 香
ei	day	sei 四
eui	no equivalent	heui 去
eun	no equivalent	seun 信
eut	no equivalent	chēut 出

I

i	bee	si 试
iu	"ee" + "oo"	síu 少
im	seem	dim 掂
in	seen	sìn 先
ip	jeep ("p" mute)	jip 接
it	seat ("t" mute)	yiht 热
ing	sing	bìng 冰
ik	sick ("k" mute)	sīk 识

O

o	orchard	cho 错
oil	boy	choi 菜
on	on	gòn 干
ong	song	tòng 汤
ot	ought ("t" mute)	hot 渴
ok	awkward	gwok 国
ou	toe	dou 到

U

u	fruit	fu 裤
ui	"oo" + "ee"	bùi 杯
un	soon	bùn 搬
ut	boot ("t" mute)	fut 阔
ung	tone	jùng 钟
uk	hook ("k" mute)	ūk 屋

YU		
yu	no equivalent	syù 书
yun	no equivalent	syùn 酸
yut	no equivalent	syut 雪

Tones

The following is a sketch illustrating the co-relation of the seven tones in Cantonese:

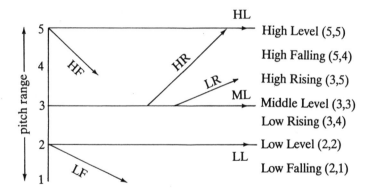

It is important to note that a sound in a certain tone may differ in meaning from the same sound in another tone. The following is an example:

Name of Tone	Tone Mark	Example
High Level	–	sī 诗
High Falling	`	sì 撕
High Rising	´	sí 史
Middle Level	none	si 试
Low Falling	` with an 'h' after the vowel	sìh 时
Low Rising	´ with an 'h' after the vowel	síh 市
Low Level	with an 'h' after the vowel	sih 事

Appendix 3
A Brief Chinese Chronology

From Xia Dynasty to Qing Dynasty

Xia Dynasty 夏			21 BC (approx.) – 16 BC (approx.)
Shang Dynasty 商			16 BC (approx.) – 11 BC (approx.)
周 Zhou Dynasty	西周 Western Zhou Dynasty		11 BC (approx.) – 711 BC
	Eastern Zhou Dynasty 东周		770–256 BC
	Spring and Autumn 春秋		770–476 BC
	Warring States 战国		475–221 BC
Qin Dynasty 秦			221–207 BC
汉 Han Dynasty	Western Han 西汉		206 BC–24
	Eastern Han 东汉		25–220
三国 Three Kingdoms	Wei 魏		220–265
	Shu 蜀		221–263
	Wu 吴		222–280
Western Jin Dynasty 西晋			265–316
Eastern Jin Dynasty 东晋			317–420
南北朝 Northern and Southern Dynasties	南朝 Southern Dynasties	宋 Song	420–479
		齐 Qi	479–502
		梁 Liang	502–557
		陈 Chen	557–589
	北朝 Northern Dynasties	北魏 Northern Wei	386–534
		东魏 Eastern Wei	534–550

	北齐 Northern Qi	550–557
	西魏 Western Wei	535–556
	北周 Northern Zhou	557–581
隋 Sui Dynasty		581–618
唐 Tang Dynasty		618–907
五代 Five Dynasties	后梁 Later Liang	907–923
	后唐 Later Tang	923–936
	后晋 Later Jin	936–946
	后汉 Later Han	947–950
	后周 Later Zhou	951–960
宋 Song Dynasties	北宋 Northern Song Dynasty	960–1127
	南宋 Southern Song Dynasty	1127–1279
辽 Liao Dynasty		916–1125
金 Jin Dynasty		1115–1234
元 Yuan Dynasty		1271–1368
明 Ming Dynasty		1368–1644
清 Qing Dynasty		1644–1911

Appendix 4
Vocabulary in Cantonese Romanization

The original complex form of the character is underlined
The character not underlined is the same in simplified form

1. 一字千金

呂不韋	Néuih Bāt Wáih
秦始皇	Chèuhn Chí Wòhng
呂氏春秋	Léuih Sih Chèun Chàu
孔子	Húng Jí
字典	jih dín
字體	jih tái
字帖	jih tip
數字	sou jih
文字	màhn jih
金屬	gàm suhk
黃金	wòhng gàm
黃金時代	wòhng gàm sìh doih

2. 一鳴驚人

齊威王	Chàih Wài Wòhng
淳于髡	Sèuhn Yù Kwàn
鳴禽	mìhng kàhm
驚動	gìng duhng
驚慌	gìng fòng
驚奇	gìng kèih
驚天動地	gìng tìn duhng deih
驚險	gìng hím
驚心動魄	gìng sàm duhng paak

3. 一鼓作氣

曹劌	Chòuh Gwai
魯莊公	Lóuh Jòng Kùng
鼓勵	gú laih
鼓足幹勁	gú jūk gon ging
作品	jok bán
工作	gùng jok
合作	hahp jok
振作	jan jok
氣量	hei leuhng
氣派	hei paai
空氣	hùng hei

4. 為虎作倀

助桀(紂)	joh Giht (Jauh)
為虐	wàih yeuhk
為	wàih
為民請命	waih màhn chéng mihng
為難	wàih nàahn
為甚麼	waih sahm mò
為生	wàih sàng
為限	wàih haahn
為主	wàih jyú
虎口餘生	fú háu yùh sàng

虎頭蛇尾	fú tàuh sèh méih
老虎	lóuh fú

5. 葉公好龍

龍袍	lùhng pòuh
好	hóu
落葉	lohk yihp
樹葉	syuh yihp
公有	gùng yáuh
好吃	hóu hek
好處	hóu chyu
好客	hou haak
好奇	hou kèih
好強	hou kèuhng
好人	hóu yàhn

6. 樂不思蜀

劉備	Làuh Beih (Béi)
蜀	Suhk
劉禪	Làuh Sìhm
魏	Ngaih
樂而忘返	lohk yìh mòhng fáan
樂器	ngohk hei
快樂	faai lohk
享樂	héung lohk
音樂	yàm ngohk
思念	sì nihm
思想	sì séung

7. 東施效顰

西施	Sài Sì
弄巧成拙	nuhng háau sìhng jyut

東方	dùng fòng
東西	dùng sài
施工	sì gùng
施行	sì hàhng
效法	haauh faat
效果	haauh gwó
仿效	fóng haauh
無效	mòuh haauh

8. 江郎才盡

江淹	Gòng Yìm
庾信	Yùh Seun
小江	Síu Gòng
江仔	Gòng Jái
江河日下	gòng hòh yaht hah
牛郎	ngàuh lòhng
女郎	néuih lòhng
才能	chòih nàhng
文才	màhn chòih
盡心盡力	jeuhn sàm jeuhn lihk
窮盡	kùhng jeuhn
無窮無盡	mòuh kùhng mòuh jeuhn

9. 自相矛盾

內部矛盾	noih bouh màauh téuhn
國際矛盾	gwok jai màauh téuhn
自己	jih géi
自覺	jih gok
自修	jih sàu
自由	jih yàuh

相對	sèung deui
相逢	sèung fùhng
相識	sèung sīk
相同	sèung tùhng

10. 守株待兔

不勞而獲	bāt lòuh yìh wohk
等待	dáng doih
侍女	sih néuih
兔子	tou jí
免除	míhn chèuih
守法	sáu faat
守候	sáu hauh
守衛	sáu waih
待業	doih yihp
期待	kèih doih
招待	jìu doih

11. 刎頸之交

藺相如	Leuhn Sèung Yùh
趙	Jiuh
廉頗	Lìhm Pó
負荊請罪	fu gìng chíng jeuih
自刎	jih máhn
交換	gàau wuhn
交際	gàau jai
交情	gàau chìhng
交涉	gàau sip
交談	gàau tàahm
交通	gàau tùng
交易	gàau yihk
交友	gàau yáuh

12. 紙上談兵

趙括	Jiuh Kwut
紙板	jí báan
紙幣	jí baih
紙張	jí jèung
談話	tàahm wah
談論	tàahm leuhn
談判	tàahm pun
兵器	bìng hei
士兵	sih bìng

13. 作法自斃

孝公	Haau Gùng
商鞅	Sèung Yéuhng
死	séi
作法	jok faat
作曲	jok kūk
製作	jai jok
法官	faat gùn
法律	faat leuht
法庭	faat tìhng
自由	jih yàuh
斃命	baih mihng

14. 完璧歸趙

牆壁	chèuhng bīk
完備	yùhn beih
完滿	yùhn múhn
完全	yùhn chyùhn
完整	yùhn jíng
璧還	bīk wàahn
歸國	gwài gwok
歸家	gwài gà

15. 杯弓蛇影

庸人自擾	yùhng yàhn jih yíu
杯子	bùi jí
酒杯	jáu bùi
弓箭	gùng jin
弓形	gùng yìhng
影子	yíng jí
電影	dihn yíng
電影院	dihn yíng yún

16. 刻舟求劍

刻薄	hāk bohk
刻意	hāk yi
雕刻	dìu hāk
時刻	sìh hāk
求婚	kàuh fàn
求學	kàuh hohk
請求	chíng kàuh
要求	yìu kauh
劍術	gim seuht

17. 圖窮匕現

燕	Yìn
荊軻	Gìng Ò
富	fu
圖案	tòuh on
圖書館	tòuh syù gùn
地圖	deih tòuh
窮盡	kùhng jeuhn
窮苦	kùhng fú
窮人	kùhng yàhn
貧窮	pàhn kùhng
匕首	beih sáu

18. 畫蛇添足

腳	geuk
畫冊	wá chaak
畫稿	wá góu
畫畫	waahk wá
增添	jàng tìm
充足	chùng jūk
滿足	múhn jūk

19. 歧路亡羊

楊朱	Yèuhng Jyù
楊子	Yèuhng Jí
忘	mòhng
忙	mòhng
芒	mòhng
路標	louh bìu
路途	louh tòuh
路障	louh jeung
出路	chēut louh
死亡	séi mòhng
羊毛	yèuhng mòuh
羊群(羣)	yèuhng kwàhn
羊肉	yèuhng yuhk

20. 南柯一夢

槐安國	Wàaih Òn Gwok
黃粱一夢	wòhng lèuhng yàt muhng
南針	nàahm jàm
夢境	muhng gíng
夢想	muhng séung

做夢	jouh muhng
夜<u>長</u>夢多	yeh chèuhng muhng dò

21. 指鹿<u>為</u><u>馬</u>

胡亥	Wùh Hoih
二世	Yih Sai
<u>趙</u>高	Jiuh Gòu
<u>顛</u>倒黑白	dìn dóu hāk baahk
手指	sáu jí
<u>腳</u>趾	geuk jí
指甲	jí gaap
指示	jí sih
<u>為</u>非作歹	wàih fèi jok dáai
<u>為</u>止	wàih jí
行<u>為</u>	hàhng wàih

22. 臥<u>薪</u>嘗<u>膽</u>

吳	Ǹgh
越	Yuht
夫差	Fùh Chàai
勾<u>踐</u>	Ngàu Chín
<u>薪</u>金	sàn gàm
<u>薪</u>水	sàn séui
高<u>薪</u>	gòu sàn
<u>膽</u>敢	dàam gám
<u>擔</u>任	daam yahm
臥病	ngoh behng
臥室	ngoh sāt
年<u>薪</u>	nìhn sàn
月<u>薪</u>	yuht sàn
嘗試	sèuhng si
<u>膽</u>大	dáam daaih

<u>膽</u>識	dáam sīk
<u>膽</u>小	dáam síu

23. 請君入<u>甕</u>

武<u>則</u>天	Móuh Jāk Tìn
周<u>興</u>	Jàu Hìng
來俊臣	Lòih Jeun Sàhn
何日君再	hòh yaht gwàn joi
<u>來</u>	lòih
陳君	Chàhn gwàn
<u>國</u>君	gwok gwàn
臣	sàhn
請願	chíng yuhn
聘<u>請</u>	ping chíng
申<u>請</u>	sàn chíng
君主	gwàn jyú
君子	gwàn jí
入<u>場</u>	yahp chèuhng
入口	yahp háu

24. 狼<u>狽</u><u>為</u>奸

忠	jùng
朋比<u>為</u>奸	pàhng bei wàih gàan
狼	hán
奸細	gàan sai
奸邪	gàan chèh
奸淫	gàan yàhm
奸<u>詐</u>	gàan ja

25. 破釜沉舟

項羽	Hohng Yúh
楚	Chó
孤注一<u>擲</u>	gù jyu yāt jaahk

鐵釜	tit fú
斧頭	fú tàuh
破壞	po waaih
破舊立新	po gauh lahp sàn
破爛	po laahn
沉迷	chàhm màih
沉沒	chàhm muht
沉默	chàhm mahk
沉痛	chàhm tung
沉重	chàhm chúhng
沉住氣	chàhm jyuh hei
沉醉	chàhm jeui

26. 驚弓之鳥

漏網之魚	lauh móhng jì yùh
驚人	gìng yàhn
驚喜	gìng héi
驚醒	gìng síng
鳥瞰	níuh ham

27. 望梅止渴

曹操	Chòuh Chòu
畫餅充飢	waahk béng chùng gèi
口渴	háu hot
喝水	hot séui
渴望	hot mohng
希望	hèi mohng
願望	yuhn mohng
禁止吸烟	gàm jí kàp yìn
停止	tìhng jí

28. 懸樑（梁）刺股

孫敬	Syùn Ging

蘇秦	Sòu Chèuhn
懸掛	yùhn gwa
懸殊	yùhn syùh
刺激	chi gìk
刺繡	chi sau
行刺	hàhng sik
股東	gú dùng
股份	gú fahn (fán)
股票	gú piu
股息	gú sìk

29. 愚公移山

智叟	Ji Sáu
公用	gùng yuhng
私	sì
愚笨	yùh bahn
愚蠢	yùh chéun
愚弄	yùh nuhng
移動	yìh duhng
移民	yìh màhn
移山倒海	yìh sàan dóu hói

30. 揠苗助長

拔	baht
長	chèuhng
幼苗	yau mìuh
汽笛	hei deht
苗牀	mìuh chòhng
苗圃	mìuh póu
苗條	mìuh tìuh
幫助	bòng joh
補助	bóu joh
長處	chèuhng chyu

長久	chèuhng gáu
長大	jéung daaih
長者	jéung jé
生長	sàng jéung
市長	síh jéung

31. 濫竽充數

吹竽	chèui yùh
竹竿	jùk gòn
芋頭	wuh tàuh
濫用	laahm yuhng
氾濫	fáahn laahm
充分	chùng fahn
充足	chùng jūk
冒充	mouh chùng
數量	sou leuhng
數目	sou muhk

32. 塞翁失馬

焉知非福	yìn jì fèi fūk
敷衍塞責	fù hín sāk jaak
塞外	choi ngoih
老漁翁	lóuh yùh yùng
失敗	sāt baaih
失手	sāt sáu
失業	sāt yihp
損失	syún sāt
遺失	wàih sāt

33. 熟能生巧

瓜熟蒂落	gwà suhk tai lohk
飯熟	faahn suhk
熟路	suhk louh

熟人	suhk yàhn
熟食	suhk sihk
熟睡	suhk seuih
熟習	suhk jaahp
能幹	nàhng gon
能力	nàhng lihk
才能	chòih nàhng
巧妙	háau miuh

34. 鷸蚌相爭，漁人得利

漁民	yùh màhn
魚乾	yùh gòn
相比	sèung béi
相稱	sèung ching
相等	sèung dáng
相信	sèung seun
獲得	wohk dāk
利息	leih sīk
利用	leih yuhng
便利	bihn leih

35. 螳螂捕蟬，黃雀在後

捕捉	bouh jūk
逮捕	daih bouh
實在	saht joih
現在	yihn joih
後悔	hauh fui
後來	hauh lòih
落後	lohk lauh

Index

A. Hanyu Pinyin

Chinese character in simplified form

B. Cantonese Romanization

Chinese character in original complex form